HOME FREE!

And life is Worth Living....

KEN COOPER

Author of *Held Hostage*

© 2018 by Ken Cooper

Published by KCPM Publishing

P.O. Box 77160, Jacksonville, FL 32226

Printed in the United States of America

All rights reserved. No part of this publication may be reproduced, stored in a retrieval system or transmitted in any form or by any means – example, electronic, photocopy, recording – without the prior written permission of the publisher. The only exception is brief quotation in printed reviews.

ISBN 978-0-692-16017-6 PAPERBACK

MUSIC LYRICS ON PAGE 6 TAKEN FROM JOHN NEWTON, "AMAZING GRACE."

MUSIC LYRICS ON PAGES 5 & 6 TAKEN FROM W.D. CORNELL AND W.G. COOPER, "WONDERFUL PEACE."

The Cover Story

The picture depicting freedom on the cover of *Home Free!* is based on the closing scene of Ken Cooper's popular book, *Held Hostage*.

Dedication

To my wife, June, and Mom who welcomed me back to freedom with the lights of home burning brightly, and to the prison ministers, chaplains and Christian inmates who helped me see the Light, Jesus Christ, when I sat, hopeless, in darkness.

To all the repentant criminals behind prison bars praying, hoping, waiting to be set home free.

Acknowledgements

I'm indebted to John Pelot, who did the final manuscript formatting, Dugger Jamison for editorial feedback and to Rebecca Cooper for proofreading.

Author's Note

I did my best to accurately describe every incident and anecdote as they happened those many years ago. Due to the time lapse since the dialogues occurred, the conversations are paraphrased at best, but I took great care to express the essence and spirit of the verbal exchanges. Please note that I *italicized* the thoughts and conversations with myself in order to invite the reader into my mind where he or she is more apt to experience my emotions.

Home FREE!
By Ken Cooper

1

At midnight when I turned onto the country road in southeastern Kentucky where Mom lived, my heart shifted into high gear. Up on the hill I could see the lights of mother's home burning brightly. *I'm home free!*

It was my first trip back to Mom's place after my release from Florida prisons where I served three years for armed bank robberies.

When I pulled into her driveway, I parked the car and with both hands resting on the steering wheel, I sat there talking to myself: *I can't believe I'm home...I was sentenced to 99 years just three years ago. When I gave my life to Christ in lockup, God began to bless me more than I deserved. That surprised me, but now...the favor the parole commission showed me...out in three on 99...unbelievable...I deserved to die in prison...home in three years. Wow! No wonder I'm at peace with the authorities. I'm on 99-year parole, but you know, Lord, I'm scared I'll violate and go back to prison for life!*

As I stepped out of the car, my spirit soared, and I shouted to the familiar poplar trees that welcomed me, "I'm a free bird...hope none of the local law, or my family try to clip my wings!"

Mother appeared in the doorway in the carport. I ran to her like a lost child who had just been found. With her arms wide open, she embraced me. Her prodigal son had returned home at last.

Despite the midnight hour, mom seemed as young as my forty-nine years as we laughed and talked about the olden days and good family times. One o'clock became two as she caught me up on news and home happenings that escaped me during my three years away from home.

When we retired for the "night," I slept like I'd gone to heaven, and at nine, woke up to the earthy aroma of frying bacon. *Wow! I am home. Mother's in the kitchen.*

After a breakfast of oven-baked scratch biscuits, fried farm bacon, scrambled eggs and homemade scuppernong grape jelly, Mom washed, and I dried the dishes. *She's almost a foot shorter than me.*

When we finished our chore that seemed like a treat, I held her tiny warm hand in mine as I led her out onto the back porch for a walk. We were headed for her vegetable garden that promised fresh corn-on-the-cob, sun-kissed, vine-ripened tomatoes and pole beans for supper.

Perched on the edge of the porch was an old wringer type washing machine. "Is this the same wringer washer that ate my seven-year-old thumb for lunch?" I asked.

"The very same one…but you were eight."

I looked at my thumb and laughed. "You have a modern type in the laundry room," I said, questioning mother as to why she would have two washing machines.

"I keep it for looks; it takes me back to many good memories…when you five boys were growing up in West Virginia…your dad working in the mines."

Not-so-good old memories flashed before me. Seven of us lived in a two-bedroom company house and we owed our souls to the company store. Dad, though usually peaceful and calm, stormed into the house on Friday nights, ranting and raging over the debt that kept growing larger and larger…his despair may have fueled my hatred for the Philadelphia bankers who owned the mines. A tow-headed "Jesse James" robbing banks with a toy handgun…

Home FREE!
By Ken Cooper

I blinked the old troubling images away, squeezed her hand and said, "I'm glad, Mom; but it reminds me how much better you have it now: away from the coal camps...independent and living alone."

She held my eyes with hers and smiled. "Your dad was a foreman at Coal Camp Number Six. I remember that many of the women carried their washing down to the creek and beat their family clothes on the rocks to clean them."

I remembered something else and laughed before releasing my hand from hers. I said, "I remember that West Virginia coal camp and you beating me down at the creek bank with a willow switch."

Mother roared with laughter.

"Mom, I'm glad you kept the washing machine...and glad you threw the willow switches away."

"My middle of five boys...you were always into everything, but the thing that bothered you the most was being accused of doing something bad you didn't do."

"I know, but I don't know if I've grown up very much…I still can't take it when people judge me for my crimes when I'm doing good now."

Mom nodded, and as we stepped off the porch, she said, "You did your time; people should forgive you and give you a second chance. All that is behind us now."

I mused to myself, *I'm home free; Thomas Wolfe was wrong. You can go home again.*

2

The truth of the moment overwhelmed me, and I felt high, higher than a high from the most powerful surge of adrenaline from robbing a bank, taking control with a toy gun. I blurted, "This quiet high is better, sweeter…"

Mother interrupted me. "The Bible calls it peace that passes understanding, my dear boy."

Before I could react, she sang a line from a song she had sung to me the one time she visited me in prison: "Peace, peace, wonderful peace flowing down from the Father above."

I turned and hugged mom. Her soft warm love reminded me of my wife, June. I squeezed Mom tighter and said, "I wish June could be home with us; I miss her so much."

Mom faced me and with the tips of her fingers she touched the golden ring on my finger. "June is another reason I think you'll stay out of trouble…make it out here, and not go back to prison."

"You mean because she'd kill me!"

With a twinkle in her eye, she stepped back and said, "For sure, but I'm thankful God gave you a wife who is a strong Christian, an independent woman who loves the Lord and you enough to talk truth to both of you."

"June really does that," I said, laughing. "What a blessing she is. She talks to God all the time, and I have peace of mind knowing she puts God first and worships Him rather than me."

Mother's eyes twinkled. "She is a woman of God, and that's the reason you have peace, peace, wonderful peace flowing down from the Father above."

Mom's energy at 73 amazed me, but I said, "Even *Wonderful Peace* sings so much better out here than in the joint."

To my surprise, rather than singing another verse of the peace song, mother belted out, "Amazing grace how sweet the sound that saved a wretch like me; I once was lost but now I'm found, was blind but now I see."

I'm found! I see! I'm home! I said to myself as I dabbed tears of joy.

Mom smiled knowingly and said, "You remember that Amazing Grace was Daddy's favorite song?"

I nodded and sat down in a white rocking chair. Mother joined me in a matching chair. I rocked to my delight and reminisced: "When I was a wee lad about eight, I sang it with him as we traveled to churches to preach," I said.

"What a beautiful picture...maybe those trips were a glimpse of God's will for your life."

"What do you mean?"

"All those scripture verses you memorized with him, all those sermons you heard; perhaps you will go out and preach like him some day."

Goose bumps rose up on my arms and a chill settled over me. "I don't know about all that. Mother, I feel unworthy to even call myself a Christian in front of people who know my past...much less being a preacher someday."

"Remember the message you received as a boy of ten?"

"Sure, I remember it well. I was playing under the oak tree outside the front yard, all alone, when a voice spoke to me in my heart, 'When you grow up you'll be a preacher like your Grandpa King.'"

Tears filled Mom's eyes; hair rose up on my neck!

To escape the uncomfortable moment, I stood up, turned to her and said, "While you do your thing, I'm going to check out the old high school and that new recreation park...I may do a little jogging."

Mother knew exactly what was happening, so she said, "Listen, son, you can call it jogging or whatever you want to, but you'll never be really free until you stop running from God!"

In that moment I didn't know if I were running from God or her, but in a flash I was out the door and in my car. If her speech wasn't enough to steal the sense of freedom I'd enjoyed to that point, as I drove toward the park about a mile down the road from mother's home, all tranquility was snatched away when a flashing blue light appeared in the rear-view mirror.

3

Unable to believe what I was seeing, I blinked, swallowed hard and felt blood leave my stomach and rush into my chest. My heart pounded like a jackhammer, and the hair on the back of my neck became electric. *It's a cop; they've come to get me, arrest me...*

My body slumped, but to control myself, I gripped the steering wheel. That seemed to help and eventually the fear that I would lose my freedom began to give way to reason. *There's no cuffs on your wrists yet, Coop; settle down.*

I pulled the car over to the side of the road. With trembling fingers, I rolled the window down and waited for the officer.

When he didn't come immediately, I mouthed my personal version of an oft used scripture verse in prison that was perfect for the occasion. *I have nothing to fear. God has given me a spirit of power and a sound mind.*

A calm feeling came over me, and in the outside mirror I watched the uniformed man approach. *It's a local sheriff's deputy, a strapping young man in a hurry.*

"Good morning, sir," he said as he leaned down and peered at me through the open window. "I stopped you to talk with you for a minute."

"Sir, I thank you for your courtesy...was I speeding, eh...breaking the law?"

"No, you weren't."

"That's a relief, sir," I said, irritated that my baritone voice sounded unusually high pitched and weak.

The young officer coughed. "Captain told us if we spotted you to pull you over and check your papers...a Travel Permit from your Florida parole officer, please." He stuck his big paw through the window.

My hand trembled as I leaned over and took the authorization paper out of the glove compartment and handed it over to him. "Here it is, sir," I said.

He studied the packet, returned it to me and said, "Cooper, you're the guy alright ... appears everything is in order...visiting your mother on East Apple Tree Road, I see, but I do have one question. How in the world was a serial bank robber set free in three years on ninety-nine?"

Dumbfounded that the deputy knew how the authorities favored me with an unheard of early release, I felt the blood leave my face, but then I managed to say, "The only thing I know, sir, is that they set me free...my mom just told me I might become a preacher like my grandpa, George King, but I don't understand the miracle of it...don't know why...but I'm really thankful for my freedom."

The deputy scratched his head. "Oh, I see, eh, so I'll let you go for now, but don't forget we've got our eyes on you."

"I understand, sir, and thanks for letting me go!"

4

As I drove away, a mixture of hilarity and adrenaline coursed through my body...If another cop stops me now, he'd give me a ticket for flying too high to drive.

Two minutes later that seemed like ten seconds, I arrived back on Planet Earth at a modern recreation complex built a little more than a "three-point hoops shot" from McCreary County High School where, as a junior, I played basketball. *Amazing that little brother Paul started while I warmed the bench. All I can see now is his fiery eyes when we met at a highway service station before I left Florida...he's right! I ruined the family name and he means it...he'll shoot me if I lay one foot on his property.*

I took a deep breath, closed my eyes and asked God for help: *Thank you, Lord, again for my freedom...for a homecoming day in Kentucky. Wish Paul could enjoy it with me...oh how much I hurt him, Mom, and a lot of others...I put them through hell. Please don't let him do anything crazy!*

I opened my eyes and looked around. To me the park appeared like paradise. Everywhere I gazed were well manicured trees, grass, red-clay basketball and tennis courts, and a green little league ball field: a virtual garden full of happy people having fun.

Strolling onto a red-clay path, I forgot about Paul and my shame. I felt as much at home and as free as the puffy white clouds chasing the sun across the sky. I stopped at a concession stand midway between the hoops court and the little league ball field down the hill.

I grabbed a Gatorade, took a sip and headed for the miniature ball park. In my ecstasy, I didn't sense that a dark tempest hovered over me and would threaten my freedom.

Oblivious to what was about to happen, I stood behind the backstop and watched preschool children play T-ball. I loved it. Tiny youngsters in uniforms two-sizes-too-huge knocked a baseball off a giant peg, scampered to the wrong base or ran into their mother's arms...in the stands. I laughed with the crowd and felt a part of them. Prison had robbed me of a sense of belonging in groups of people outside the fences that had separated me from them for three years. And in lockup, I really missed mixing with families, especially young parents with little kids.

As I laughed, a peace like I felt at Mom's settled over me. But the calm feeling was short-lived.

Out of the corner of my eye, I saw a man scrambling from the bleachers. He rushed toward me, his face bloodred as he stormed me like a raging bull. He raised his fist and blasted me, "What are *you* doing here?"

I was taken aback. A supercharge of adrenaline coursed through my body; my muscles tightened, my mouth dropped open, but no words came out.

His contorted face and clinched fists told me he was dangerous...maybe like Paul. The shot of protective juice kicked me into a higher gear and energized my whole body but not my brain as he screamed a second time. "I asked *you* a question! What are *you* doing *here*?"

My body was on high alert, my face turned from pale pink to crimson. My right arm twitched, but somehow, I managed to not lose control, stepped back and studied his enraged eyes...eyes that were angry, piercing, fiery.

When words finally came, I stammered, "I-I-I'm watching kids play T-ball."

"Oh no, you're not!" he shouted, jerking a long thumb toward the parking lot. "You're outta here, mister!"

Anger mixed with indignation pumped a third charge of adrenaline into my bloodstream; the hair on my neck stood up, but again I held my composure. My inner man knew why I couldn't lose control and act out with anger even if my body didn't. I was on ninety-nine-year parole, absolutely determined to not be violated and shipped back to prison to die. It would take just one lapse. One mistake and I'd go back for life. I bowed my head, humbled myself, threw up my hands in what must have looked like surrender to a prison guard and muttered, "Why?"

"You're Cooper, aren't you?" he bellowed, growing louder with each word.

"Yes, I am," I whispered. That's when I figured...like the small-town cop, he recognized me as the bank robber Cooper recently released from prison.

My manly pride and rage gave way to reason: *I'd better get out of here before he does something really crazy.*

Like a scolded inmate banned from the rec yard by an angry guard for no reason at all...and forced to return to his cell, I inched past him toward my car.

The man-child monster within me was raging, so it shocked me that I was leaving. But it shocked me even more to hear the words that unexpectedly came out of my mouth when I turned back to him and said, "I'm going, but I expect to see you in a church pew tomorrow." He appeared as shocked as I was.

As I drove away, I replayed the look of astonishment on his face and laughed about the strange words I'd spouted, "...see you in a church pew tomorrow."

5

To say I was reluctant to attend church the next morning would be a gross understatement. Given the guilt I felt for shaming my family and the hard feelings I harbored toward the young man, I felt unworthy to go to a place of worship...and I would undoubtedly have to face accusers, friends of my family, who would condemn me for my crimes...for ruining the family name...with their cold eyes, if not with their harsh words.

But when I passed through the door into the room where the men's Sunday School class met, the only thing I saw were two vacant chairs in a circle of a dozen men. I eased over to the seat closest to the door and sat down. When I raised my head, my body tingled. All eyes were on me. I flashed back to the "spotlight" where the FBI interrogated me regarding the banks I had robbed.

The teacher attempted to rescue me. "Welcome, Kenneth! Welcome! I'm Denzil King. I taught your older Cooper brothers, Jim and Ted, in school. We're glad you're here."

Wish I were, I thought. Not knowing what to say, I acknowledged his kind words with a nod.

At that moment a man walked through the door and looked for a vacant seat. He came over to take the chair next to me. As I looked up into his face, my eyes must have bugged out. It was the young man from the T-ball field. He was red-faced, and his body seemed to stiffen before he exhaled deeply and plopped onto the chair beside me.

I sat there absolutely amazed, traumatized, trying my best to not burst out in laughter at what was happening, but I didn't succeed totally. I turned my face from his. A slight smirk widened into a crescent-shaped smile that soon stretched from ear to ear. It seemed to me that nobody but God himself could manipulate circumstances like this. That notion led to the thought that God was a "character" of sorts and was getting his kicks out of demonstrating his power in a bizarre way. The man, who had judged, embarrassed and threatened me, was indeed in church with me and forced to sit right beside me.

I loved the moment and held my hand over my mouth to keep from expressing my shock and glee. The weird words spoken to the red-faced man as he forced me to leave the ball field had come true. *I'll see you in a church pew tomorrow. I figured*

Home FREE!
By Ken Cooper

I'd attend church with my mom, but I certainly didn't dream my prediction would come true.

With a sneaky sideways glance, I noticed that the face of the man beside me had turned into a scarlet frown. He was upset and uncomfortable. He fidgeted in his chair. In fact, we both fidgeted our way through the class discussion. The dual theme for the lesson was "Forgive and you shall be forgiven." And "Judge not and you shall not be judged." When I heard this I was certain that the entire episode had been orchestrated by none other than our Father in Heaven who knew the hearts of two of his unforgiving, judgmental children.

It was amazing. My amazement turned into astonishment as the day continued. The whole experience was apparently God-directed. The timing was ingenious. The plan was perfect. It was a heavenly conspiracy that had just begun.

6

When I made my way back upstairs, the second part of the heaven-initiated plot was addressed by my Sunday school-teacher-mother: "This Sunday is Holy Communion Day, son."

In my silence, Mom read my troubled mind and said, "Don't fret; it's a day when each one who partakes of the Lord's Supper comes face to face in a special way with their sins."

A grunt of horror escaped from my gut, but I didn't say anything. Mother cleared her throat and continued, "Each person is given an opportunity to make things right with God and their fellowman."

The red necktie Mother bought me for the occasion seemed to suddenly tighten around my throat. Ready for the hanging, I could barely swallow. *This is a conspiracy. I hate "my fellowman" from the ball field.* I squirmed in the pew next to my unsuspecting mother, wondering what else God was up to.

As the Communion elements were served to the congregation I bowed my head and wept. But the weeping came from an anger that kept me from forgiving and praying for the man who had rejected, humbled and embarrassed me the day before. Nevertheless, in that moment I felt an internal cleansing may have begun. By the time the service ended with the traditional parting hymn, a feeling that I was okay with God and most of his children came over me.

That assurance caused me to forget the conspiracy theory that, to humble me, God was working on me big time. I felt more lighthearted all day as my mom and I shared lunch and visited relatives on my deceased father's side. There was not an ounce of condemnation in any of them. They had apparently forgiven me. I felt really free and noticed that I was eager to get back to church for the evening service.

Given the bizarre two-part drama of the morning, however, I eased onto the back row and sat with Uncle Dean, Mother's kid brother who was barely two years older than me.

Just before the service began, though, the pastor came back and asked me to move up to the very front row. I looked at him like he was crazy, but then stood up. He escorted me to the privileged pew at the front of the church. My blood pressure rose, and I braced for the worst. My eyes darted to the place he indicated, then to the people sitting there next to the vacant spot. I was to sit on the aisle at the end of the first pew. Beside me would be two children. Seated on the other side of them was their father...the young man from the T-ball field!

My jaw dropped, and I hurriedly clamped it shut, took a deep breath and sat down. My pulse quickened, and my knees knocked. I questioned God, *I don't know what you are up to now, Father. Where's the wisdom in this...you surely don't want an ugly scene here? On the front row? In church?*

As I prayed for self-control, all I could think about was the anger the young man exploded with at the T-ball game. Anxiously I pleaded with God: *Father, is this where the axe will fall? Are my days of freedom numbered? About to be cut off?*

Finally, I dismissed those wild fear-thoughts and asked God to take control, but agonized that he wouldn't as scenes of brutal conflicts in prison flashed back and kicked in a super charge of adrenaline. As I had learned to do facing prison authorities, I fixed my eyes on the pastor and locked my hands between my knees to keep them from trembling, though somehow, I kept one eye on the man down the row.

The first move came from the pastor, who stood up to begin the evening service. I released my hands from the knee lock and sat upright. After the traditional introduction that reminded me of my Grandpa King, the pastor asked everyone to take off their shoes and socks. "Tonight's our biannual foot washing," he announced.

A weird unknown feeling came over me. My feet were suddenly cold and the rest of my body hot. I jerked a look across the room at Mother. Her mouth formed a firm line and she nodded at me. I took off my shoes and socks, thankful that neither sock was holey. *Holey socks for an unholy man.* I smiled at that boyish thought, turned, and looked down the pew to focus on the angry man who sat with bowed head. I smiled again. His white feet were as long as the long fellows of a lanky basketball player. *He's no different or better than me.* It bothered me that I was comparing him to myself, and worse yet, I was judging him.

The pastor must have known my heart. He carried a basin of water and placed it in front of my feet. My body stiffened. I was astounded. *Someone is going to wash my feet! This is not right!* A feeling of unholy embarrassment came over me and I crossed my feet: uneasy, unsure if I wanted someone to wash my feet. *Am I worthy or confused that I would even submit to a foot washing? Much less wash someone else's feet? This is as bad as it gets.* But it wasn't.

7

Things got worse. The pastor looked down and eyed the pew where I was sitting, motioned toward me with his hand, waved at the youthful father down the way, and instructed him to "wash Brother Kenneth's feet." Goosebumps ran the length of my body and I swallowed a lump in my throat. I hadn't told anyone about the previous day's incident. Only God and my adversary knew.

Now, that same man who was forced to humble himself and sit with me in Sunday school class had been instructed to wash my feet. I was overwhelmed by the pastor's words to the youth, and the authoritative command *"Wash Brother Kenneth's feet!"* washed around and around in my inner being. I felt dizzy but glanced at the young man's face.

Before he stood, his youthful countenance became old with deep wrinkles that told me he had died a thousand deaths. I wondered what he would do. He gulped twice, clutched the edge of the church bench and raised his body to face his pastor.

Trembling he turned, stumbled toward me, and took his place in front of me. As he knelt at my feet, he wept.

I wept, too, took a deep breath and looked down at my feet. He could have washed them with the river of tears streaming down his face. My whole body trembled. It was all I could do to sit there. I wiped the tears from my eyes and peeked at his children. Their eyes were large. They began to weep. Their faces were bright with confusion *or is it fear*...as they watched their father mourning, tenderly holding my feet and pouring water over them.

The warm water—his warm hands scooping the soothing liquid on my cold feet helped me calm down and brought a feeling of inner warmth I had never felt before. It seemed that he was washing much more than my feet. He was washing away the hatred, the hurt, the shame and pain...rejection...out of me...out of my spirit. He was doing something for me I couldn't do for myself.

When he finished, he stood and returned, barefooted, to his seat, snuffing, wiping tears. The pastor motioned to me and said, "Now, wash Brother Larry's feet." *Now, it's my turn.*

I eased by the children, slumped to my knees in front of him, lifted and placed Larry's feet in the warm water one foot at a time. I could have washed his feet with my tears. Through the watery mist I caught a glimpse of God. A deep love and compassion I had never experienced welled up in me and consumed me in that precious moment. Shaken to the core, my hands trembled, and what seemed like an eternity later, when I finished washing his feet, I dried them with a huge white towel.

As I stood up, to my surprise, he arose and faced me. His countenance beamed. We lunged into each other's arms. It was a brotherly bear hug I'll never forget. Runny noses and tears wet our shoulders. I didn't care that we were making a mess. All the hurt feelings I held for him, Paul, and others who had rejected me because of my crimes drained out of me. And the Lord filled me up to overflowing with his love and forgiveness.

I thanked God for what he had done and exclaimed, "I'm free!"

THE END

Epilogue
......*31 years later*

The young man serves as a pastor.

Ken Cooper serves as a prison minister.

Ironically, the young man's name was Watters.

"TO ERR IS HUMAN; TO FORGIVE, DIVINE."
-Alexander Pope

It can be difficult to forgive others, especially when they've done horrible things to us. Jesus Christ forgave everyone, even the people who tortured and nailed Him to the cross! Though not easy, we are to follow Him in forgiving others.

If you've struggled with forgiving one or more people (or even yourself), here's a prayer you could consider. It matters not how you word your prayer, only that you are truly asking and forgiving.

Dear Lord,
I thank You for Your power of forgiveness, and I choose to forgive those who have wronged me. Help me forgive [name anyone who has hurt you] and I release them to You as Romans 12:19 tells us to do. Help me to bless those who have hurt me as you have commanded in Romans 12:14. I choose to be kind and compassionate and to forgive others, just as You forgive me, Lord. In Jesus' name I ask this. Amen.

Home FREE!
By Ken Cooper

The Roman Road
The Sinner's Path to Salvation

We are all sinners by nature and our own actions - Romans 3:23:
"For all have sinned and come short of the glory of God."

All of us deserve punishment, but God offers something else - Romans 6:23:
"For the wages of sin is death; but the gift of God is eternal life through Jesus Christ the Lord."

God sent His son, Jesus, as the sacrifice for our sins - Romans 5:8:
"But God commandeth his love toward us, in that while we were still sinners, Christ died for us."

We only need to accept God's gift, and in return, we give Him our lives - Romans 10:9-10:
"That if thou shalt confess with thy mouth the Lord Jesus, and shalt believe in thine heart that God hath raised him from the dead, thou shalt be saved. For with the heart man believeth unto righteousness; and with the mouth confession if made unto salvation."

God assures us of our salvation – Romans 10:13:
"For whosoever shall call upon the name of the Lord shall be saved."

Home FREE!
By Ken Cooper

Would you like to be saved? Are you ready to accept Jesus Christ as your Savior?

1. We can't earn salvation; it's a gift from God.
2. We are saved by God's unequaled grace.
3. Believe you are a sinner and that Christ died for your sins, then ask His forgiveness.
4. Turn from your sins—this is what we call repentance. Jesus Christ knows you personally and loves you personally. What matters to Him is the attitude of your heart and your honesty in accepting Him.

There are no special words, but we suggest praying the following prayer to accept Christ as your Savior:

"Dear God,
I know I'm a sinner, and I ask for your forgiveness.
I believe Jesus Christ is Your Son.
I believe that Jesus died for my sins and that you raised Him to life.
Commitment:
I trust you, Jesus, as my Savior. Come into my heart and fill me with your Spirit!
Please live and love through me as my Lord that your will and my will may be one.
I pray this in the name of Jesus.
Amen."

Home FREE!
By Ken Cooper

HOME FREE!

$3.00

Proceeds benefit KCPM, Inc.

a 501(C)3 tax exempt prison ministry.

Order printed copies:

KCPM Publishing

P.O. Box 77160, Jacksonville, FL 32226

Order e-copies:

Visit: www.kencooperministries.org

For free copies land-mailed to prison chapel libraries and individual inmates:

KCPM Publishing

P. O. Box 77160

Jacksonville, Fl 32226

For information and to contact the author:

Email: coop3631@bellsouth.net

Website: www.kencooperministries.org

Telephone: (904) 859-9780

www.ingramcontent.com/pod-product-compliance
Lightning Source LLC
Chambersburg PA
CBHW030313030426
42337CB00012B/696